BENJAMIN ZEPHANIAH is one of Britain's most renowned poets.
By the time he was 15 he had gained a reputation as a young poet
who was capable of speaking on local and international issues.
His first book, *Pen Rhythm* (Page One Books) was published when
he was 22. Throughout his career, his mission has been to take poetry
everywhere and to everyone. In 1998 the University of North London
awarded him an honorary doctorate in recognition of his work.
His previous poetry collections include *Talking Turkeys*,
Funky Chickens and *Wicked World* (Puffin). He has
also written two novels: *Face* and *Refugee Boy* (Bloomsbury).
His other book for Frances Lincoln is *J is for Jamaica*.

PRODEEPTA DAS is a freelance photographer and author
whose pictures have been published in over 20 children's titles.
In 1991 *Inside India*, which he also wrote, won the Commonwealth
Photographers' Award. His previous books for Frances Lincoln
include *I is for India*, *J is for Jamaica*, *K is for Korea*,
Geeta's Day and *Prita Goes to India*.

We Are Britain!

Poems by Benjamin Zephaniah
Photographs by Prodeepta Das

FRANCES LINCOLN

Kenny

ISLE OF HARRIS

Helen

SCOTLAND

Jordan

GLASGOW

OMAGH

N. IRELAND

Jialu

Zachary

LEEDS

Sam

NOTTINGHAM

NORWICH

WALES

ENGLAND

Jajar

Liam

BLAINA

SEVEN KINGS

TWICKENHAM

Sevda

LONDON

PLYMOUTH

Michael

Hannah and Rebecca

Prita

Benjamin Zephaniah

Who are the British?

**Ask us, and you will find that we dance to
music from America, Africa and Asia;
we eat food from Ireland, Italy and Jamaica;
we speak more than three-hundred languages
and we know over four-hundred different ways
to cook a potato. We look Celtic, Arab and Bengali;
we wear kilts, saris and football shorts; and if you get
very close to us and look right into our eyes, you can
almost see the history of the whole world.**

**This book takes a poetic look at thirteen young British people
as they work, rest and play. None of these children want to live in
a world where everybody looks like them; they are all ready
to embrace a multicultural, multicoloured land where every child
is equal and all children have a poem to call their own.
If Britain is going to be great in the future, it will be because
these kids want curry and chips, mangoes and strawberries
and banana crumble, and they think of all these as British.**

**The British are not a single tribe, or a single religion, and we
don't come from a single place. But we are building a home
where we are all able to be who we want to be, yet still be British.**

That is what we do: we take, we adapt, and we move forward.

We are the British. We are Britain!

Sam lives in Norwich and his favourite places are Four Stairs, the Law Courts and the Sainsbury Bridge. Why? Because they're all fantastic for skateboarding. Four Stairs is best because it's good for doing ollies (jumps).

As soon as he turns 16, Sam wants to work in a skateboarding shop. His other hobby is going up the climbing wall at his local sports centre.

His mum is French and his dad is Melanesian, from the Solomon Islands.

The Economy Flyer

You will need a good plan
If you want to catch Sam —
He's the skateboarding man.

Watch him as he flies by,
Getting busy so high,
Skateboarding through the sky.

It doesn't matter where,
He will take to the air,
People will stand and stare.

Yes he moves with the times.
Every now and then he climbs
And he likes to rap rhymes.

He flies through the scene
Like a flying machine,
He is so quick and keen.

He just cannot conceal
How exciting it feels
When he's speeding on wheels.

He will never retire —
This economy flyer
Just gets higher and higher.

You really must see
Sam defy gravity —
It is quite heavenly.

Trees Please

Prita likes climbing trees
She does;
Prita likes climbing trees.
Up sycamores and English oaks,
You can find Prita telling jokes.
Upon the chestnut tree's big roots,
You can find Prita eating fruits.
Up apple trees where apples grow,
Prita and friends are known to go.
She likes to climb a big hawthorn
That lives next to a big acorn.
Prita likes climbing trees
She does;
Prita likes climbing trees.

One night Prita had a dream
About a tree that grew ice-cream,
But when she woke up the next day
The ice-cream tree melted away.
Now what she really wants to see
Is an orange-flavoured chocolate tree.
Meanwhile she will always climb
When school is over and she has time,
Because
Prita likes climbing trees
She does;
Prita likes climbing trees.

Prita lives in East London

Prita lives with her elder sister Amrita and her mother and father, in Wanstead on London's eastern fringe. Prita's parents come from eastern India and she was born in London.

She follows the teaching of Ramakrishna, a Hindu saint, and does *japa* (meditation) every morning and evening.

Prita enjoys feeding a squirrel called Chestnut who visits her garden from Epping Forest. She also likes cooking, riding on buses and winding her sister up. She wishes milk and bananas had not been invented as her mum is always insisting that they are good for her!

Jialu lives in Leeds

Jialu wants to be a pop star, but will she ever find the time? She's always so busy drawing, doing origami, swimming and playing. She loves jelly, chips, and *jiaozi* (dumplings), sometimes all at the same time!

Her family comes from China and that's where she was born, but she now lives in Leeds. Her best friends Lucy and Yilin are also her neighbours.

As well as playing lots, Jialu never stops smiling. It has been said that she even smiles when she's sleeping.

A Reason For Seasons

In the spring Jialu loves playing
When the flowers start to bloom,
In the park and in the playground,
In the kitchen and her room.
She talks to passing butterflies
And if a bird's in song,
She knows just how to harmonise
And so she sings along.

In the summer Jialu loves playing —
She loves summer a lot.
She plays tennis and goes swimming
When the sun shines very hot.
She runs up hills, she runs down hills,
Sometimes she runs round and round.
When she gets too hot she eats jelly —
It helps to cool her down!

In the autumn Jialu loves playing
As the leaves begin to fall.
When smart squirrels start to store food
She's out playing with her ball.
When the days start to get shorter
And the weather's not so kind,
Jialu finds it hard to keep still —
She's got good times on her mind.

In the winter when it's freezing
And there's bright white snow and ice,
Jialu simply starts believing
That the weather's very nice.
She thinks seasons are amazing,
She plays each day of the year.
She thinks life is meant for playing,
She thinks that is why she's here.

Sevda Has a Brother

Sevda has a brother –
She thinks he's a delight.
She woke up to discover
That he was born one night.
Her father thinks he's pretty,
Her mother thinks he's smart,
And Sevda thinks he's witty
And quite a work of art.

Sevda's celebrating –
She thinks her brother's great,
So Sevda is creating
A large, sweet Kurdish cake.

But mother's telling Sevda
That it is her belief
That if she's really clever
She'll wait till he has teeth.

Sevda has a brother –
Her family has grown,
And how they love each other
In their North London home.
This lovely brand new baby boy –
Bilal is his name –
Has filled young Sevda's eyes with joy,
Life just won't be the same.

Sevda lives in North London

Sevda and her family are refugees from Kurdistan. Her family is Muslim and her mum teaches her the *Koran* – the sacred book of their religion. Sevda enjoys playing board games with her little brother and sister and her best friend, who is also from Kurdistan.

Like nearly all children, Sevda loves watching TV. She especially likes Turkish films and the Teletubbies! Her favourite food is *dolma* – meat, rice, tomato and yoghurt wrapped in vine leaves.

Liam lives in Blaina, South Wales

Liam lives in Blaina, South Wales. At the back of the house lies the 'jungle', a wooded area where only children are allowed. He plays games there after school with his friends.

Liam lives in an old mining area – all the coal mines have closed down now. He goes fishing in the local pond which used to be used for washing coal. He also likes strumming his toy guitar and playing rugby with his Dad.

King of the Jungle

Liam is king of the jungle -
The jungle in South Wales.
The one at the back of his yard -
And life in the jungle is hard.

Liam is king of the jungle,
This is no fairytale.
The jungle can be very rough,
But Liam and his friend are tough.

Liam is king of the jungle,
King over all that he sees.
He was going to be a coal miner,
But now he's the greatest tree climber.

Liam is king of the jungle,
He talks to the birds and the bees.
Adults say, "The jungle is wild,"
But he's an intelligent child.

Liam is king of the jungle,
He's kingly but very polite.
Liam don't care if it's raining,
You'll never find this kid complaining.

Liam is king of the jungle,
But when it gets dark and it's night,
Liam goes home to get fed,
And sleep in his nice cosy bed.

Hannah and Rebecca Rhyme

Hannah and Rebecca
Were growing up together,
When Hannah and Rebecca
Discovered poetry.
So Hannah wrote a letter
To her sister Rebecca
Which said,
"Hey my big sister
Why don't you rhyme with me?"

Rebecca wrote to Hannah
In a quite poetic manner.
She studied English grammar
So she knew just how to rhyme.

She said,
"We must stick together
No matter what the weather.
Have no doubt whatsoever,
I'll rhyme with you anytime."

So they're now writing a poem
That just will not stop growing,
And wherever they are going
That poem goes there too.
Now their rhymes just keep on flowing
And their love just keeps on showing,
So it's really worthwhile knowing
If somebody rhymes with you.

Hannah and Rebecca live in Twickenham

Hannah and Rebecca both like playing the piano, reading and wrestling! They are the founders of a magazine for children called *SMART*, which they write and edit themselves.

Their mother came to Britain from Croatia, and their father came from Hungary.

This is a vegan family, which means they eat no meat, fish or dairy products. They really enjoy having big family meals together, which are followed by Hannah and Rebecca playing their favourite reggae records and doing some rather crazy dancing!

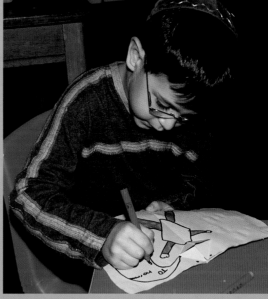

Every Sunday, Zachary goes to Hebrew classes at the Progressive Jewish Synagogue. There he learns about Jewish religion, culture and traditions.

In his spare time he enjoys riding his bike along the riverside, going to basketball club and learning the drums.

But most of all Zachary likes practising magic. When he grows up, he wants to be a famous escapologist so his parents will have to spend a lot of time looking for him.

Zachary is happy
When he's doing magic,
His dad said he can make a rope
Float in the air.
When he's doing magic
There's no need to panic,
Even when he makes his dad's coat
Disappear.

Visit him
You won't leave –
He has tricks
Up his sleeve.
He can make time wait,
Tie his hands
And he'll escape.
Even when he's in bed
He does tricks in his head.
With a playing card or two,
This kid will
Amaze you.

Zachary is happy
When he's doing magic,
Every time he does a show
People wonder how.
When he's doing magic
He's defying logic;
The ladies and the gentlemen
who see him
All go,

Magical is He

"Wow!"

The Legend

The legend of the Isle of Harris
Has spread throughout Bangkok and Paris.
The legend has spread low and high –
The legend of Kenny MacKay.

He grows from seeds and ploughs the land,
The girl next door thinks he is grand.
The neighbours and birds in the sky
Wave to him when he passes by.

This Gaelic boy is brave and bold.
He doesn't seem to fear the cold.
The weather causes no delay –
He loves to go to school each day.

And even when he has exams,
He's quickly home to feed his lambs.
The legend says he's full of power
That he obtained from cauliflower.

He's hard working and doesn't fear.
He's happy when he does his share.
He sure knows how to use a pen,
He has the strength of many men.

The people say there is no malice
Upon the bonny Isle of Harris.
They say they are protected by
The legend of Kenny MacKay.

Kenny lives on the Isle of Harris in Scotland

Kenny lives on the Isle of Harris off the north-west coast of Scotland, with his mum and dad, two big brothers and little sister.

Kenny's dad's family have been crofters on the island since the 19th Century. It's very difficult to grow things there because of the harsh weather conditions.

Kenny has five pet lambs and a sheep dog. He feeds the lambs milk every morning before school, and then again when he comes home. He also helps out by driving the family's tractor to prepare the fields for cultivation.

Kenny loves football – he supports Glasgow Rangers – and he also likes riding his bike around the island in his spare time.

Helen lives in Omagh, Northern Ireland

Helen lives on the outskirts of Omagh, in Northern Ireland. Her parents drive her into town to school every day. Her head-teacher is really nice and friendly and she gives the children sweets when they're good.

In her spare time Helen loves Irish dancing and she plays the piano and violin, too. She's also into swimming, chicken chow mein and playing hide-and-seek! When she grows up, she wants to be a lawyer.

The Dancer

Like a butterfly she dances by,
Playing in the air,
Glowing in the light,
Reminding us that rhythm
Is what life is made of.

She is a magnificent idea
Brought to life by loved ones
On violin and piano.
She is what we all dream of being –
Graceful, hopeful,
Joyful and in harmony.
That's why when the birds and bees
come out,
They look on with pride.
They recognise beauty,
They know sweet sunshine.

If only she was everywhere,
Her laughing eyes,
Her smiling feet.

If only we could all see her at once.
If everyone had the pleasure
It would happen.
Mountains could be moved,
Lightning would be tamed,
And paint would turn into flowers.

Just look at her go,
Just look at her flow.
Helen can do it children –
Helen can increase the peace.

The Pizza Eater

His parents feed him rice and peas
And fancy looking greens.
Sometimes they give him nuts and seeds
And various string beans.
They also give him channa dhal,
Tomato soup and pike,
But Jajar just says loud and clear,
"It's pizza that I like!"!

His father said, "Son, eat your sprouts
And you'll be big and strong."
Jajar said, "Yes I'll eat them,
But I won't eat them for long."
His mother said, "Look at your Dad –
He eats a lot of meat."
Jajar just said, "Dear Mum and Dad,
It's pizza that I eat!"

Well Jajar does eat greens – he said
He knows that they are good.
He does eat chips and rotis
And fruits just as he should.
But experts have made studies,
And the experts have all found
That Jajar Sandhu's favourite food
Is very flat and round

Jajar's a pizza eater
An eater that eats pizza,
And when he eats his pizza
He drinks about a litre.
Although he lives in Essex
(that's not far from the sea),
Jajar Sandhu's favourite food
Comes from Italy!

Jajar lives in Seven Kings, Essex

Jajar's mum and dad come from the Punjab in India, and his religion is Sikh. Every week he goes to the local *Gurdwar*, the Sikh place of worship. He likes listening to the priest reading from the Holy Book, the *Granth Sahib*.

Jajar enjoys playing football with his friends in the park, but sometimes dogs chase the ball and he doesn't like dogs at all. Jajar is also into Monopoly (especially when he's the banker), corn on the cob and, of course, pizza. He has a big sister, Deedar, whom he annoys by arguing with her – and the angrier she gets, the more he argues!

Michael lives in Plymouth

Michael's grandad came from the Caribbean island of Grenada and he played cricket for the British Overseas Airways Corporation. He cooked potatoes as no one else could – particularly Michael's favourite dish, made from potato, butter and fish.

Michael plays cricket for his school. He especially enjoys having a game on Plymouth seafront, where Sir Walter Raleigh was playing when news of the Spanish Armada was brought to him.

When he was little, Michael was called the 'bug boy' because he's really interested in nature and wildlife. He has a dog called Millie, a cat called Bunni and a mouse. The dog and cat used to fight all the time, but now they just ignore each other.

Michael and Millie live together
Happily by the sea,
With a cat and a mouse
In a ship shaped house
They live in unity.
Michael has a brother and sister,
Millie's best friend is a frog,
Michael's parents are called Mrs and Mr,
And by the way,
Millie's a dog.

Millie says "Woof",
Michael says "Wow",
Millie says "Do"
And Michael says "How?"
When at the park
And Michael's playing cricket,
Millie will bark
And chew Michael's wickets.

The House of Fun

Millie says "Ruff",
Michael says "Cool",
Millie says "Shoo"
And Michael goes to school.
Michael wants to be
A cool acrobat;
Millie wants to be
As cool as a cat.

Michael and Millie live together
Happily by the sea,
With a spider called Bug
Who lives under a rug
Near a big fellow called Busy Bee.
For most of the day
These creatures just play,
They scream and they jump and they run.
None of them bite,
So Michael's all right,
Every day all they do is have fun.

RISE AND SHINE

Jordan likes karate,
He likes to play football.
He likes to swim,
He likes to grin,
He likes to do them all.
He likes eating healthy food
That's made with love and wheat,
But what he doesn't like to do
Is go to bed and sleep.

He said, "It's such a waste of time,
I could be having fun,
I could be playing with my cat
Or laughing at my mum."
He wants to exercise his mind -
Anything instead
Of getting slow and sleepy,
And spending time in bed.

Painting people, mathematics,
Feedings swans and acrobatics,
Playing football with Natasha,
He thinks she's a lovely sister.
His best friend Lee loves Jordan's style,
He loves the way he grins and smiles.
Natasha thinks he's learning Dutch -
He thinks his sister sleeps too much.

Jordan likes playing music,
He's an intellectual.
He likes to read
And to succeed
He's quite incredible.
Each day is an adventure,
No mountain is too steep.
And still he wants the world to know
He doesn't like to sleep.

Jordan lives in Glasgow

Jordan lives in Glasgow and plays the guitar. His big sister is called Natasha and he has a cat called Pikachu.

Jordan likes football (he supports Glasgow Rangers), swimming, painting people, karate, elephants and maths. He doesn't like sleeping, though, and thinks his sister sleeps too much. He wants to be busy all the time, so he doesn't mind getting lots of homework. His mum and dad's family are from the Punjab in India, Scotland and the Caribbean.

First published in Great Britain in 2002 by
Frances Lincoln Limited, 4 Torriano Mews,
Torriano Avenue, London NW5 2RZ

First paperback edition 2003

British Library Cataloguing in Publication Data
available on request

ISBN 978-0-7112-1902-1 paperback

Design by Lora Sykes

Printed in Singapore

9 8

MORE PICTURE BOOKS FROM FRANCES LINCOLN CHILDREN'S BOOKS

Geeta's Day
Prodeepta Das

Geeta's day begins as most children's do: she washes,
brushes her teeth and has her breakfast. But when she sets off
for school, passing the *kamar* at his forge, the *bhandari* shaving
a customer and the *mali* waving garlands of flowers, her world
begins to beat to the distinctive rhythm of Indian village life...
Prodeepta Das's delightful dawn-to-dusk journal will
encourage young readers to compare and contrast
Geeta's day to their own.

ISBN 978-0-7112-2024-9   £5.99 PB

I is for India
Prodeepta Das

From *bullock cart* to *peacock*, from *namaskar* to *tea*,
here is a celebration of India in all its colourful diversity.
In this photographic alphabet, Prodeepta Das introduces
young readers to some of the customs, different religions
and forms of culture which can be found all over this
unique, vibrant subcontinent.

ISBN 978-0-7112-1101-8   £5.99 PB

J is for Jamaica
Benjamin Zephaniah
Photographs by Prodeepta Das

From *Cricket* to *Pumpkin*, from *Hummingbird* to *Yam* –
this is a photographic alphabet showing Jamaica in all its
colourful diversity. In vibrant rhyming verse, Benjamin Zephaniah
explores some of the sights, sounds and tastes of Jamaica,
from the bustling capital of Kingston, to the peaceful and serene
Blue Mountain. A perfect way to introduce children to this
small and beautiful Caribbean island with a big heart.

ISBN 978-1-84507-401-2   £10.99 HB

**Frances Lincoln titles are available from all good bookshops.
Prices are correct at time of publication, but may be subject to change.**